THE RESERVE BANK
= A License to Steal Money from Citizens?

How Money Is Created from Nothing for Dummies

A. Motiar

Strategic Book Publishing and Rights Co.

Strategic Book Publishing and Rights Co.
12620 FM 1960, Suite A4-507
Houston TX 77065
www.sbpra.com

ISBN: 978-1-62516-529-9

Dedicated to:

The community of volunteers and activists at:

"The New Economic Rights Alliance" <www.newera.org.za>
in South Africa,

"Hopegirl2012" <http://hopegirl2012.wordpress.com/>

and

"The THRIVE Movement" <http://www.thrivemovement.com/>
in the United States,

and

Individuals all over the world,
who are taking up the challenge to address the injustices
imbedded in the present monetary system,
and thereby bring an end to the oppression of the financial elites
who have made perpetual debt-slaves of the citizens where they
operate.

* * * * * * *

It is worth remembering:

*"...it does not require a majority to prevail, but rather an
irate,
tireless minority keen to set brush fires in people's minds."*

– Samuel Adams

Updated segment from the book

"Condoned Injustices"

which was short-listed for the R50,000 Penguin Book
Award

THE RESERVE BANK
= A License to Steal Money from Citizens?

(How money is created from nothing for dummies)

Discover:
 ➢ *How the Reserve Bank creates money out of thin air*
 ➢ *How the "fraud" game is played by the Reserve Bank*
 ➢ *How the Reserve Bank depletes YOUR money*
 ➢ *Organizations working to change the status quo*

"If the people only understood the rank injustice of
our money and the banking system,
there would be a revolution before morning."

– Andrew Jackson: President of the United States

CONTENTS

1. PRIMARY REFERENCES USED FOR THIS BOOK

THE RESERVE BANK
= A License to Steal Money from citizens?

"Understanding how our current monetary system works to enslave us is the key to finding out how we can liberate ourselves from a modern form of tyranny,

secretly imposed upon us by the bankers which is designed to drive us into bankruptcy or debt slavery."

Excerpt from "Zeitgeist Addendum," 2008 Documentary film

Primary References used for this book were obtained from the following sources:

- *Global Outlook* Magazine: Collector's Edition, www.GlobalOutlook.ca, Issue 13, 2009.

- Bill Still & Pat Carmack, *The Money Masters,* DVD, www.GlobalOutlook.ca, 1998

- *Monopoly Men*, DVD, www.GlobalOutlook.ca, 1999

- *"Zeitgeist Addendum, "* www.GlobalOutlook.ca, 2008

- Zeitgeist - The Movie: Federal Reserve, http://www.youtube.com/watch?v=_dmPchuXIXQ

- The documentary "THRIVE": http://www.thrivemovement.com/the_movie

I am deeply grateful for the information provided by the authors of the above material.

2. INTRODUCTION

"The money power [referring to the Bank] preys upon the nation in times of peace and conspires against it in times of adversity."

– Abraham Lincoln:

16th President of the United States

* * * * * * *

The "**Occupy Wall Street**" protest movement *(OccupyWallSt.org)* was an eye-opener for most people. For the first time, citizens began to closely examine many of the injustices imbedded in the operations of the major banks and financial houses. It was painful for citizens to find their hard earned tax dollars were being used to bail out the most-wealthy institutions of the country that misappropriated funds. The financial crisis created by the banks had the most painful impact on average citizens who had no part in creating the crisis in the first place. The **Federal Reserve Bank's** role in this disaster cannot be underestimated, as it played quite a significant role in facilitating the immoral activities of the banks, which resulted in those massive bailouts by government. In 2011, one top European banker in Switzerland even admitted that **they** "engineered the global financial crisis."[1]

While the Reserve Banks in most countries play a very pivotal role in the monetary policies and economies of the respective countries, many people are unaware of how these banks control the **creation** and **issuing of money**. Hence, there is an urgent need to examine the nefarious role of the **Reserve Bank** because humanity is suffering and will continue to suffer until the deeply flawed and iniquitous monetary system is changed.

The aim of this booklet is therefore to offer an exposition of the workings and activities of the Reserve Bank that is simple and easy to understand.

To obtain some insight of the Reserve Bank of a given country, (with its apex being the *Bank for International Settlements* in Basle, Switzerland [2]), it would be most revealing to examine the objectives of the "founders" of the Federal Reserve Bank of the United States for establishing such an institution. Glenn Beck of Fox News, [3] in an interview with author G. Edward Griffin,[4] recounts how the founders sat around the table in 1907 on Jekyll Island in the United States, and hammered out the details for what later became the Federal Reserve Bank. They came about with **FIVE** key objectives. These were:

1. To **stop** the growing **competition** from the nations' newer banks.

    *In other words, create a "**cartel**" made up of banks belonging to those who were meeting on Jekyll Island.*

2. To obtain a **franchise** to **create money out of nothing** for the purpose of lending.

    *It must be noted here that they were seeking an "**exclusive**" franchise for themselves.*

3. To **get control** of the reserves of all the other banks.

    The supposed explanation was to prevent "reckless" banks from exposure to currency drains or bankruptcies – as if they were going to be any less "reckless" as history has shown them to be. In fact, they have also turned out to be extremely ruthless.

4. To **shift the losses** from the bank owners to the taxpayers.

    What a cunning way to protect their own assets and guarantee profits!

5. To **convince** the United States Congress that the purpose is **to protect the public**.

    What a scheming strategy to persuade the Government to grant them their "exclusive" franchise.

None of these audacious objectives can be considered to be in the best interest of the citizens of the country. Moreover, as "protection," they wanted the government to come in as a **partner** to use the nation's police and military forces if required to ensure citizen compliance of their diabolical scheme. One would think no government would be willing to accept these five objectives as it would result in that country becoming enslaved to the bankers through perpetual debt. However, over the objections of the members of the Republican Party, **President Woodrow Wilson**, having a majority of the Democratic Party in Congress in 1913, granted the Charter that created the **Federal Reserve Bank,** which is today able to operate <u>with no government oversight or accountability</u>. However, later when he was out of office, President Wilson publicly lamented about his action to create the Federal Reserve Bank.

Not surprisingly, the handful of founders and their representatives who met on Jekyll Island and drafted those objectives, are today the **owners** of the major banks in the United States, and also have, in some cases, controlling interests in many Central/Reserve Banks of other countries around the world. There can be no doubt in anyone's mind that the major purpose of these bankers' desire to obtain such control, was to achieve their far reaching goal to *"dominate the political system of each country and the economy of the world as a whole."* Professor Carroll Quigley of Georgetown University, states:

> "The powers of financial capitalism had another far reaching aim, nothing less than to create a world system of financial control in **private hands** able to <u>dominate the political system of each country and the economy of the world as a whole</u>. This system was to be controlled in a feudalist fashion by the central banks of the world acting in concert, by secret agreements, arrived at in frequent private meetings and conferences. The apex of the system was the **Bank for International Settlements** in **Basle, Switzerland;** a private bank owned and controlled by the worlds' central banks which were themselves private corporations. The growth of financial capitalism made possible a centralization of world economic control and use of this power for the **direct benefit** of **financiers** and the **indirect injury** of **all other economic groups.**"[5]

3. THE PYRAMID OF CONTROL

The pyramid presented here from the documentary "THRIVE" [6] shows how a handful of bankers as the *Financial Elites* have succeeded in their efforts to **DOMINATE** the political system of many countries and the economy of the world as a whole.

"The **global domination agenda** is a plan by powerful private bankers to take over all our primary systems (money, energy, food, media, etc.) and to establish a sole global authority – with themselves in charge. They use the media, central banks, multinational corporations, governments, major foundations, and international agencies such as the IMF and World Bank to implement their strategies. So far they have successfully brought down countries across the globe, including Argentina, Chile, Ecuador, Argentina, Tanzania, Indonesia, Brazil, Poland, Mexico, Bolivia, Thailand, Iceland, the Soviet Union, Japan, Greece and scores of others. They are now attempting to dismantle the U.S. by collapsing the dollar and making sure Americans are in debt they can't repay.

"This pyramid shows the basic structure of control. The financial elite are at the top. They use international and national central banks to control corporations (which they loan to at special rates), manipulate national economies and hence their governments, and **get everyone in debt to the bankers.**

"Regular working people, who produce most of the real wealth on this planet, are at the bottom of the pyramid. As of 2007, the richest **2%** of adults owned more than **50%** of the global assets and as of 2010, <u>one out of every seven people didn't have enough to eat</u>.

"Material wealth and resources continue to funnel up to the financial elite, while domination and control come down through the international banking structure and the corporations and governments below them. It's important to note that the strength of the pyramid is in its base. As people wake up and withdraw their support, the corrupt money structure will lose its control." [7]

"The Pyramid of Control" from THRIVE:

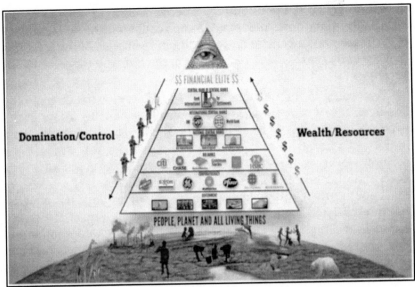

FINANCIAL ELITES
Central Bank of Central Banks:
Bank of International Settlements
↓
International Central Banks: IMF & World Bank
↓
Federal Reserve Banks
↓
Big National Banks
↓
Corporatocracy
(Control through multinational corporations)
↓
Governments
↓
People Planet and Living Things
(Regular working people)

The arrow on the right of the *Pyramid of Control* depicts the flow of **"resources"** from the bottom to the top.

The arrow on the left of the *Pyramid of Control* depicts the assertion of **"control"** from the top to the bottom.

15

We are living at a critical time when we are going through one serious economic crisis after another, which impact far more devastatingly on the poor and the middle class than they do on the rich. Sadly, many government laws and regulations have a tendency to facilitate the concentration of wealth in the hands of the few. This inevitably increases the divide between the rich and the poor in our society.

According to the documentary, _THRIVE_, "The current economy has been taken over by a **rigged** system that benefits a few at the expense of most . . . The **_Economics Sector_** is perhaps the most important one of all to **transform** because the way the money system works, it directly impacts each and every person's job, home, family and community. Creating centralized banks, a system that requires debt and makes up money out of nothing, has allowed the international banking elite to gradually turn almost the entire world into a population of **debt-slaves**. Exposing and eliminating this system – and replacing it with an honest and open one can provide the critical turning point toward creating a world where all can thrive." [8]

4. WHO CREATES MONEY AND WHERE IS THIS MONEY STORED?

In order to "**unslave**" citizens from the debt-cycle, first, one has to understand how the system is "**rigged**." This is the only way one is ever going to change the current situation for the majority of the citizens to succeed and prosper. So let's begin with the simple question:

Who creates money and where is this money stored?

When this question is asked to graduates who have Economics or Bachelor of Commerce degrees, the common answer one often gets without a blink of an eyelid is, "The Government creates the money and it is stored at the Reserve Bank."

The follow-up question is, "Who owns the Reserve Bank?"

Again, the instant response quite often is: "**The Government**."

While thankfully this may not be the view of all people, sadly this is a common but widespread understanding of many including those who are students of Economics, businessmen and even those who work in banks. What most people do not realize is that the **Reserve Bank** is a **privately-owned institution**.

They find this to be incredulous!

Let's take the example of one of the large Reserve Banks in the world, the "**Federal Reserve Bank**" of the United States. This is a good place to start as most Reserve Banks in the so-called capital "free-market" countries are based on a somewhat similar model. To offer a simple means to prove it is a private corporation, one need only to consult the local Telephone Directory. All American government agencies and departments are in the special government blue pages of the Directory. Anyone searching for the *"Federal Reserve Bank"* in the blue government pages of the Telephone Directory would be frustrated as it will not be found there. It is not there because it is not part of the government.

A. Motiar

However, one would easily find the <u>Federal Reserve Bank</u> in the regular white pages, in the same place where one would find the private courier service, *"Federal Express."*

You might find this surprising, considering that it was the President of the United States who "announced" the appointment of Ben Bernanke as the new Chairman of the Federal Reserve Bank. This was done amidst great anticipation – by President Bush during his term in office – as everyone wanted to know who the President would name to be the successor of Allen Greenspan, the outgoing Chairman. Here again, we notice a great "con-game" played on citizens by the private owners of the Federal Reserve Bank.

To maintain the **"impression"** in the public mind that the Federal Reserve Bank is a government institution, the ***private owners*** of the Federal Reserve Bank, hand over to the President of the United States a few names from their own slate of "private" owners. Hence, contrary to perception, the President does not independently appoint the "best person" for the post from the large pool of American citizens who are highly qualified for this responsible position. He is merely **assigned the task** by the Federal Reserve Bank, to select and announce the name of one of the candidates on the list given to the President. This announcement is done from the Oval Office, amidst great media hype and fanfare, with the whole country glued to their T. V. screens, to learn who would be the new Chairman of supposedly "their" Federal Reserve Bank.

This sleek media operation is cleverly orchestrated to give the impression to the general public that the newly announced Chairman is *"their"* Chairman of *"their"* Federal Reserve Bank. Nothing can be further from the truth. It must be noted though that the Chairman of the Reserve Bank or the Governor as in South Africa, though shouldering considerable responsibilities, is the "public" face or the spokesperson for that country's Reserve Bank. The ultimate decisions are done behind closed doors by the bank's power elite – the select group of private shareholders and directors.

5. THE RESERVE BANK

To establish that the **South African Reserve Bank** is also a private institution, in 2009 I sent the following query letter to the South African Reserve Bank. To make it easy for them to respond, all questions were structured to require only a "yes" or "no" answer.

Reserve Bank: Media Desk

> I would appreciate it if you would kindly provide me with answers for the following questions. To make it easy for you, I have phrased most of the questions where possible requiring you to simply insert a "YES" or "NO" answer beside each question. You are however free to elaborate on any answer if you so wish.

1. Does the Reserve Bank have an arms-length relationship with the government?

2. Can the Government influence the governance or policies of the Reserve Bank?

3. Can the Government dictate the rate of interest the Reserve Bank sets periodically?

4. Does the Government own all the shares in the Reserve Bank?

5. If the answer to the above question is "NO," then would it be correct to say that the Reserve Bank is a private corporation with no government control over it?

6. Does the Reserve Bank have share holders?

7. Does the Reserve Bank have institutions (like Banks) as share holders?

8. Does the Reserve Bank have individuals as share holders?

9. Are the Reserve Bank's majority share holders Banks/institutions?

10. Are the Reserve Bank's majority share holder's individuals?

11. Does the Reserve Bank issue dividends to its shareholders?

12. Can the public buy shares in the Reserve Bank?

As one of the most important institution in the country, where does one get more information about the role and function of the Reserve Bank?

Your prompt response to the above questions would be highly appreciated.

A. Motiar.

Received the following Response:

Your Query has been received by the SA Reserve Bank and has been assigned to a responsible person. A response will be sent to you as soon as possible. Your reference number for this query is 31584EXM.

To date, **no further response has been received** for the questions I asked, even though the response required for most questions was a simple YES or NO answer, with the option to elaborate on any answer if they so desired.

Can one conclude that the South African Reserve Bank, like many other Central/Reserve Banks in the world is a **private** institution?

6. HOW MONEY IS CREATED AND EXPANDED?

To return to our main question. If the government does not create the money, then who does?

The Reserve Bank does!

The immediate questions that arise are:

1. But if the Reserve Bank is a private corporation, how can a "private" corporation issue money?

2. Where does it get the money to make those huge loans?

The Federal Reserve Bank creates money from "**nothing.**" It simply uses some very sneaky maneuvers to vaporize money from thin air. Confused? Most people usually are if they don't know the "**fraud-like**" game that is played by the Federal Reserve Bank. In fact, the Reserve Bank promotes this confusion to detract people from closely examining its operations. It does so by using jargon and obfuscating charts that make it difficult for most people to understand and interpret. Understandably, the Reserve Bank is not desirous to expose the fraudulent method by which it expands the money supply.

To explain it in lay man's terms, this is how the Reserve Bank creates money from "nothing." Presented here is a simplistic model to help clarify the process. This applies to all **"privately-owned"** Reserve Banks whether they deal in dollars($), pounds(£) rand(R) or other national currency. Suppose the Government needs **10 billion rand**. Where does it go to obtain it? Their most desired option is usually the Reserve Bank – the supposed "storehouse" of all the country's finances.

Now, for the purpose of this example, let's assume that the Reserve Bank coffers are **empty**. For the "honest" law-abiding citizen that would be a problem because where on earth does one get such a huge sum of money to give to the Government if one's coffers are empty. For the Reserve Bank that's not a problem. In fact, the Reserve Bank is delighted by this request. It is ready and most willing to provide the money in **exchange** for 10 billion rand's worth of **Government Bonds**. Remember, a "bond" is an instrument of "**debt**" – *money owed which has to be paid back by a certain due date.*

Now, the government takes some pieces of paper, puts some designs on it, calls them "**Treasury Bonds**," puts a 10 billion rand value on them, and sends it over to the Reserve Bank. *(Government Bonds are like promissory notes where the issuer of the bond promises to pay back the face value of the bond plus interest over a stated period of time.)*

The folks at the Reserve Bank, now get their own, even more impressive pieces of paper, put more elaborate fancy designs on it, label them "**Reserve Bank Notes**," and also attach a 10 billion rand value to them. Note, so far there is no "real" truck loads of money that is exchanged. It's all paper transactions.

The Reserve Bank then **trades** its *Bank Notes* for the *Treasury Bonds*. The Government now takes the 10 billion rand *Reserve Bank Notes* and deposits them into its own Bank account. Once the *Reserve Bank Notes* are deposited into a Bank account, they officially become "**legal tender**" money; that is, real 10 billion rand money the government can withdraw from the bank and spend it for government works and other needs. *("Legal tender" means that the Reserve Bank note is considered a **valid and legal offer of payment**. Think of the paper check you deposit in the Bank and receive real cash money in return to make your purchases.)* By this rather simple maneuver, 10 billion rand is created out of nothing and is now added to the country's money supply.

So by this process of what is termed "**legal tender**," 10 billion rand of real **new money** has been "**easily created**" by the Reserve Bank. This is done through the purchase of government **bonds**, with money it virtually created out of thin air, using a fancy designed "*Reserve Bank Note*" that has **no real monetary deposit to cover it**. What a clever **scam!** Imagine a fancy designed "*Reserve Bank Note*" is accepted as "**legal tender**" money. It can be cashed for its face value and have no legal consequences, in spite of the fact that it has **no supporting funds** to back that "*Reserve Bank Note*." This is equivalent to someone issuing a personal check with no money in the bank account to cover it. In legal terms, this is considered "**fraud**."

Remember, for this example, we began with the Reserve Bank coffers being totally <u>empty</u> and now through this cleverly designed scam, the Bank has 10 billion rand in its coffers.

For one becoming aware of this swindle, it is natural to ask: "Why is it that the Reserve Bank can issue its '**Reserve Bank Note**' *(equivalent to a personal check)* <u>without any money</u> in its vaults, and be accepted as **legal**, but for the individual to issue a **check** <u>without having money</u> in one's bank account is unacceptable, and deemed to be **illegal?**"

Also, why is it that if an individual were to issue a check without having enough money in one's bank account, the person would be guilty of **fraud**, – *an attempt to steal money from the bank* – face prosecution, and could very likely go to prison? Yet, when the Reserve Bank, which citizens consider as the *bastion of integrity*, engages in this same "<u>illegal practice</u>," it is **not** prosecuted for **fraud**.

Is this illegal practice of the Reserve Bank not "equivalent" to stealing citizens' money?

On the contrary, its "**fraudulent**" scam is given acceptance as being "<u>legal</u>" and it is **legitimized**. Hence, the observation by <u>President Andrew Jackson</u> of the United States who said,

"If the people only understood the rank injustice of our money and the banking system, there would be a revolution before morning."

7. THE FRAUD OF INTEREST

Money is created out of debt, usually through loans from a bank and is required to be paid back with **accrued interest**. This is where the fraud becomes most manifest: Consider: When all the money is borrowed from the Reserve Bank and expanded through loans, then, only the "**principal**" is created in the money supply. If that is the case, then where does one get to cover the "**interest**" that is charged?

The simple answer is, it is nowhere to be found, because **it does not exist.** "The ramifications of this are staggering; for the amount of money owed back to the banks will always <u>exceed</u> the amount of money that is available in circulation. This is why **inflation** is a constant in the economy for new money is always needed to help cover the <u>perpetual deficit</u> built into the system <u>caused by the requirement to pay</u> **interest**.

"What this also means is that mathematically, **defaults** and **bankruptcies** are literally <u>built into the system</u>. There will always be poor pockets of society that get the short end of the stick. An analogy would be a game of musical chairs, for once the music stops, someone is left to dry.

"That's the point. It invariably <u>transfers true wealth from the individual to the banks</u>, for if you are unable to pay for your mortgage, they will take your property. This is particularly enraging when you realise that not only is such a default inevitable due to the fractional reserve practice, but also because of the fact that the money the bank loaned to you **didn't even legally exist** in the first place." [9]

What makes it even more infuriating is that through this "fraud," it seems the Reserve Bank is able **to steal the wealth of the nation**, and as a "private" institution, it is able to massively *enrich its private shareholders*. Hence, we find the South African Reserve Bank is so flushed with this easy-made money that it is able to pay its appointed directors as much as **R70,000** [10] for attending each meeting. This is more money than many in South Africa are able to earn in a year! Nowadays, in order to bring the government on board to continue to offer its blind support and also ensure their co-operation, it is also allotted some Reserve Bank shares.

However, the Reserve Bank "fraud" becomes even more interesting, creative, and ingenious when one takes a closer look at the *"Fractional Reserve System"* – a money-churning "ponzi" scheme invented by the Reserve Bank. In the example cited earlier, the **10 billion rand** deposit made by the Government in the form of Treasury Bonds, instantly become the Reserve Bank's **"reserves,"** and so do all other deposits made into this Bank.

To lend out more money, in Reserve Bank Notes of course, under their current operational model, the Reserve Bank is required to hold **10% of the transacted amount** as a **"reserve"** in its account. In the example of the 10 billion rand transaction, the Reserve Bank would hold a small **fraction of 10%** of the 10 billion rand as a "reserve." This amounts to **1 billion rand**. The remainder of the **9 billion rand**, under this cleverly devised *"Fractional Reserve System,"* is considered as **"excessive"** *reserve* and can be used as the basis for **new loans**.

"Now, it is logical to assume that this 9 billion is literally coming out of the existing 10 billion (rand) deposit. No, it does not. What really happens is that this supposedly "excessive reserve" of 9 billion is again simply created out of thin air as *Reserve Bank Notes* **on top of the existing 10 billion (rand) deposit**. This is how the money supply is **expanded**." [11]

Essentially, what the Reserve Bank does when it "makes loans is to accept promissory notes *(loan contracts)* in exchange for credits *(money)* into the Reserve Bank's transaction account." [12]

To graphically demonstrate how the *Fractional Reserve System* operates, see the **chart** on the following page. It shows how the Reserve Bank "honors" a request for a **10 billion rand** loan and uses the "multiplier effect" of the Fractional Reserve System to increase its assets from **zero rand** to as much as **R100 billion** as shown in the example provided on the chart.

8. HOW RESERVE BANK (RB) CREATES/EXPANDS MONEY FROM NOTHING

How Reserve Bank (RB) creates/expands money from nothing

A▼	B▼	C▼	D▼
New Money Created out of thin air is **9 times** the 10% Reserve on Hold in Column **D**	Reserve Bank (RB) Receives (Credits)	RB **Balance** from money Created out of thin air	Holds **10%** of **"NEW"** money created from thin air as a "reserve": **9** times this amount is then available for new loans

STARTING BALANCE OF RESERVE BANK: R 0 (or $, £, € etc.)

(a) ⟶ Government & Corporations trade their **Bonds** worth R10 billion for **RB Notes** worth R10 billion	In **exchange** for RB Note of R10 billion, RB **receives** bonds worth R**10 billion** (Credits) ⟶	From R**0** the RB now has R**10 billion** (worth of credits created out of thin air)	Holds 10% of R10 bn = R**1 billion** as a Reserve. **Nine times** this amount is then available for new loans **without any assets to support these loans.** See Column **A (b)**
		New RB Balance = R **10 billion**	
(b) ⟶ **9 x R1 billion** = R **9 billion** Created out of thin air for **New** Loans	When R **9 billion** is paid back:	+ 9 billion	Holds 10% in reserve = R**900** million. **Nine times** this amount is then available for new loans. See Column **A (c)**
		New RB Balance = R **19 billion**	
(c) ⟶ **9 x R900 million** = R **8.1 billion** Created out of thin air for **New** Loans	When R**8.1 billion** is paid back:	+ 8.1 billion	Holds 10% in reserve = R**810** million. **Nine times** this amount is then available for new loans. See Column **A (d)**
		New RB Balance = R **27.1 billion**	
(d) ⟶ **9 x R810 million** = R **7.2 billion** Created out of thin air for **New** Loans	When R**7.2 billion** is paid back:	+ 7.2 billion	Holds 10% in reserve = R**729** million. **Nine times** this amount is then available for new loans. See Column . . .
		New RB Balance = R **34.3 billion** ≫ ≫ ≫	

↓ ↓ ↓ ↓

As this process is continued, the Reserve Bank is able to create more and more money out of thin air > > > R90 **billion** (**+ R10 billion**)

9. EXPLANATION OF COLUMNS AND ROWS ON THE CHART

Column A (a) on Chart: [*Column* "A ▼" : *Row* "a →"]

To borrow money, say worth a total of **R10 billion** from the Reserve Bank, Governments and Corporations issue "**bonds**."

*Remember, bonds are like <u>promissory notes</u>, where the issuer of the bond promises to pay back the face value of the bond – in this case R10 billion, **plus** the stipulated accrued interest over a stated period of time.*

Column B (a):

The Reserve Bank is not at all alarmed that it has no money in its vaults; it simply creates a *Reserve Bank Note* on fancy designed paper, "**assigns**" a R10 billion value to it, and **trades** it in exchange for the "bonds" that are credited into its own account. (Thus, R10 billion is created out of thin air!)

Remember, a Reserve Bank Note does not have any **equivalent monetary deposit or asset to support it** *as it is <u>created out of thin air</u>. However, it is accepted as "<u>legal tender</u>" money and can be deposited in a bank for hard cash.*

Column C (a):

Starting with a **zero rand balance**, the Reserve Bank now has **R10 billion** worth of credits. This is derived from the Government or Corporation *bonds* it received in exchange for its **R10 billion** *Reserve Bank Note.*

*The "Reserve Bank Note" is simply a "note" <u>printed on fancy paper</u> that shows a face value of R10 billion. This is like waving a magic wand and presto! a **R10 billion** balance is created in the Reserve Bank's account out of thin air! (It is reasonable to ask how the Reserve Bank's action is different from what a Counterfeiter does.)*

27

Column D (a):

Under the *Fractional Reserve System*, the Bank is allowed to create more money **out of thin air**. This is done by simply placing a small *"fraction"* **of 10%** of its reserves on **hold**, and then gives itself the right to lend out money that is equivalent to **9 times** the "10%-amount" it has put aside on hold.

On the chart, this process is repeated in Rows (b), (c) and (d) to demonstrate its escalating impact *(or multiplier effect)* to increase the Reserve Bank's wealth. By using this *Fractional Reserve System (or "Scam,")* the Reserve Bank is technically able to indefinitely use this cycle of creating money from nothing. In the example given on the Chart, the Reserve Bank is able to create as much as R90 billion on top of the original R10 billion, totaling R100 billion from just one transaction of this value.

The amounts calculated in this chart do not include the accrued **interest**, which would further escalate the speed at which the Reserve Bank would be able to create its wealth out of thin air, from one original loan. Consider, how many such original transactions are made regularly, and the "multiplier effect" of each loan, enables the Reserve Bank to create further additional **billions of rand out of thin air**. *(For the Reserve Bank, each loan is like a Golden Goose that keeps on laying golden eggs.)*

As pointed out earlier, if any citizen were to write a check without having any funds in the Bank, one would be guilty of **fraud**, and liable for prosecution. Under the *"Fractional Reserve System,"* the Reserve Bank, despite **having no funds in its vaults**, lends out money in the form of a **Reserve Bank Note** that is equivalent to **9 times** of the **10%** amount it holds in reserve. In this way, it creates money from nothing, and despite its fraudulent nature, does not face any prosecution for its **"easy-made"** money.

10. WHAT GIVES MONEY ITS VALUE?

First, let's clarify the difference between "real" money and "counterfeit" money. From a moral and truly just perspective, at its very basic and simplistic level, it can be defined as follows:

- **Real money** is backed by goods or services or solid assets. It is therefore **"hard-earned"** money and is deemed to be <u>legal</u>.

- **Counterfeit money** is <u>NOT</u> backed by goods or services or solid assets. Hence, this is **"easy-made"** money and is deemed to be <u>illegal</u>.

What gives the Bank's newly created "<u>easy-made</u>" money its value, is the money that already exists and is in circulation. Unfortunately, this diminishes the value of the existing "<u>hard-earned</u>" money supply and causes **inflation**.

The **Reserve Bank's** "easy-made" money, created out of thin air, can be compared to a **Counterfeiter's** "easy-made" money, which too, is created out of thin air through the printing of notes. When counterfeit money circulates and becomes entrenched in the money supply chain, obviously – like the Reserve Bank's "easy-made" money – it diminishes the value of the real money that is in circulation. For this reason, when the <u>Counterfeiter's</u> "easy-made" money becomes exposed, the authorities/banks take very swift action to take it out of circulation. Ironically, nothing is done to remove the <u>Reserve Bank's</u> **equivalent** "easy-made" money of printed notes from circulation. That being the case, the questions that need to be answered are: Why is this so when . . .

(a) Both the **Reserve Bank's** and the **Counterfeiter's** "easy-made" money are created from thin air by simply printing notes.

(b) Both the Reserve Bank's and the Counterfeiter's "easy-made" money diminish the purchasing power of the country's currency.

29

(c) Both the Reserve Bank's and the Counterfeiter's "easy-made" money contribute to **inflation** because they are both created out of thin air and **not** backed by goods or services or any solid assets.

(d) Both the Reserve Bank's and the Counterfeiter's "easy-made" money are simply printed on good quality pieces of paper with denominated values.

(e) Both the Reserve Bank's and the Counterfeiter's "easy-made" money primarily enrich a small circle of insiders – the Reserve Bank's private shareholders, and the Counterfeiter's close associates.

(f) The primary <u>victims</u> of both the Reserve Bank's and the Counterfeiter's "easy-made" printed money scam are the innocent **citizens**.

The above facts clearly indicate the **similarities** between the Reserve Bank's and the Counterfeiter's "easy-made" money scams, which make citizens the primary **victims** of their rip-off. That being the case, the "easy-made" money of both groups is fraudulent and morally untenable. More grievously, it has a very severe negative impact on the economy of the country. Unless people are deliberately kept in the dark, citizens considering the "similarities" would rightfully wish to know why the *Reserve Bank Notes* are made acceptable as "legal tender" money and are considered <u>legal</u>, but the *Counterfeiter's Notes* are (rightfully) made <u>illegal</u>, when both notes have the same negative impact on the economy and defraud citizens?

United States Congressman **Ron Paul** clarifies the insidious nature of **inflating currency** from thin air.

> "They *(the banks)* don't say they <u>*debase the currency*</u>; they don't say they <u>*devalue the currency*</u>; they don't say **cheat the people with savings**, no, they say **lower the interest rates**. The real deception is when we distort the value of money, when we create money out of thin air, we have no savings, yet there's so-called capital . . . So my question boils down to this: how in the world can we expect to solve the problems of inflation – <u>that is the increase in the supply of money</u> – with more inflation?" [13]

Of course it cannot be done! This is because, "the Fractional Reserve System of monetary expansion is inherently inflationary.

For expanding the money supply without there being a proportional expansion of goods and services in the economy, will always **debase** the economy." [14] This becomes glaringly clear when one examines the value of the American dollar which has been devalued by as much as 96% since the Federal Reserve Bank came into existence in 1913. In other words, the purchasing power of the United States' one dollar bill in 1913 is today worth only 4 cents because of the Fractional Reserve System's Machiavellian "Ponzi" scam of creating money out of thin air. This should be a sobering thought for all citizens whose governments allow the Reserve Banks of their country to be in private hands.

Also, let's not forget that because the **Treasury Bonds** are instruments of "**debt**," they have to be redeemed before a stated due date. It may be interesting to note that the Reserve Bank, the supposed **bastion of integrity**, while projecting to be the **guardian** of the nation's wealth, provides loans to the Government (and other institutions) using "**unsecured**" pieces of fancy paper, called *Reserve Bank Notes*, but wants payment to be made in real money *(in the form of credits)* **plus "interest.**" In the example on the preceding chart, the Reserve Bank receives payments into its empty vaults from the government or other institutions that would total not only 10 billion rand, but also the additional percentage of interest (not included on the chart) that is levied on the Treasury Bonds. So by this simple con-game, the Reserve Bank is so ingeniously and efficiently able to vaporize even more money from nothing!

Using the "72" formula to double principal, *[72 ÷ (% of Interest) = Number of Years to **double** the Principal)*, a compounded interest rate of 6% requires 12 years for the principal to **double** itself. Consider the wealth creation potential when the R10 billion in our example is compounded at a 6% interest rate doubles to R**20 billion** in 12 years. Not a bad increase considering the Reserve Bank began with zero rand in its coffers.

Now, the multi-billion rand question is: Who **owns** this newly created money? Obviously, the "**private shareholders**" of the Reserve Bank, made up mainly of banks, selected individuals, and a small number of shares allotted to the government to maintain its acquiescence and support. If one considers the billions banks, institutions, and governments borrow regularly from the Reserve Bank, one can imagine the vast amount of money the Reserve Bank is able to "vaporize" from thin air to <u>enrich the private shareholders</u> of the Reserve Bank – money which rightfully belongs to the **citizens of the country** or the **Government.**

> **Is this "Ponzi" scam not a license to steal money from the citizens of a country?**

This is why it is often said by those who understand the workings of the Reserve Bank, that those who **own** the Reserve Bank are able to **"influence"** the government, and **"control"** the major assets of a country's economy. This became quite evident to the United States' President **James Madison** who exposed the danger of this convergence by warning Americans:

> *"History records that the money changers have used every form of abuse, intrigue, deceit and violent means possible to maintain their control over government by controlling money and its issuance."*

Through their ABSOLUTE monopoly on setting the rate of interest, the executive members of the Reserve Bank are placed in a strong position to **"influence"** the government, and dictate the economic policy the country is required to follow. Here again, the economic policies the Reserve Bank most desires, are those that have a direct benefit for its own private shareholders. This was clearly demonstrated during the recent economic crisis, when other countries were dropping interest rates to alleviate hardship on their consumers, the South African Reserve Bank was increasing them. This clearly **exposed** the Reserve Bank's primary consideration was the profit these higher interest rates would generate for its own **private shareholders.** It shamelessly disregarded the terrible hardship this imposed on the vast majority of the immensely poor citizens of the country. Cries of outrage from the poor were totally ignored. In justifying the higher interest rates, it was most audacious for the then Governor of the South African Reserve Bank to declare that higher interest rates hurt the rich more than they did to the poor. [15] Any average school student could tell that this was patently untrue.

If the Government of South Africa emulated the wise action of the American President Andrew Jackson, who **abolished** the Central Bank, it would not have to borrow money **"on interest"** from the Reserve Bank – money which already belonged to the Government! The billions the Government could save from a **debt-free system** could pay for:

- The expansion plans of Eskom, the South African electricity supplier, without the consumer, especially the poor, having to pay the **heavy increases in electricity rates** which Eskom is always seeking to impose on citizens; or
- A **free medical health plan** for the whole country without substantially increasing taxes; or
- **Building subsidized housing** to meet the needs of millions who do not have decent shelter; or
- Improving the **transportation infrastructure** without compelling citizens to pay steep e-tolling fees on inner-city roads; or
- **Eliminating all mud schools**, improve those that are falling apart, and provide the additional classrooms and teachers required to end the terrible over-crowding in many schools.

The list is endless. Most important of all, the government would not be in the deep **debt** situation that it is in currently. It would not have to go cap in hand to borrow from the **Reserve Bank** as it is presently constituted or other international agencies, often at above average interest rates. In the end, it is the taxpayers who have to foot the bill through increased taxes.

(Every country would have their own priority needs that could be more easily addressed by abolishing their privately-owned Reserve Banks.)

And where would one think is the headquarters of the Reserve Banks of the world? Obviously where "secret" Swiss Bank accounts are held – where some of the very rich stash away their money to avoid paying their proportion of legitimate taxes. Ironically, it is also the place where Dictators, Drug lords, the Mafia and corrupt Government officials have their secret accounts. "The apex of the system was to be the Bank of International Settlements in Basel, Switzerland; a private bank owned and controlled by the world's central banks which were themselves private corporations.... **The key to their success**, said Professor Quigley, was that the *international bankers would control and manipulate the money system of a nation* **while letting it appear** to be *controlled by the government*." [16] See Pyramid on Page 15.

Sir Josiah Stamp, Director of the Bank of England (in the 1920s), reputed to be the 2nd wealthiest man in England at that time said:

"Banking was conceived in iniquity and was born in sin. The bankers own the earth. Take it away from them, but leave them the power to create money, and with the flick of the pen they will create enough deposits to buy it back again. However, take it away from them, (i.e. the power to create money) and all the great fortunes like mine will disappear and they ought to disappear, for this would be a happier and better world to live in. But, if you wish to remain the slaves of bankers and pay the cost of your own slavery, then let them continue to create money." [17]

This statement, coming from the **Director of the Bank of England** offers one of the most compelling justifications for the abolition or re-structuring of Reserve Banks as they are presently constituted. **Professor Carrol Quigley**, the late Georgetown historian, pointed out that:

"The Reserve Banks' secret is that they have annexed from governments, monarchies and republics, the power to create the world's money on debt-terms requiring tribute both in principal and interest." [18]

This provides good insight to the comment made in 1791 by **Baron Mayer Amschel Rothschild**, the European Central Banker, who said:

"Allow me to issue and control a nation's currency and I care not who makes the laws." [19]

The question that readily comes to mind is the one **Ian Woods**, the Editor and Publisher of *Global Outlook* magazine asked:

"Why should a nation with the power to create money give that power away to a private monopoly of banks and then borrow it back at interest to the point of near bankruptcy?" [20]

This question so far remains unanswered. Ignorance of the mechanizations of the Reserve Bank may be one clue. Weak governments unable or unwilling to challenge the system, or their lack of understanding of the monetary system, may be another answer. One reason why there is not much public discussion of this

THE RESERVE BANK = A License to Steal Money from Citizens?

issue is because many colleges and universities that teach economic courses, do not have the "**money-creating mechanizations**" of the Reserve Bank that <u>usurps the public assets</u> as a topic in their textbooks or their curriculum. Discussion of the Reserve Bank is confined to an understanding of its role as a supposedly independent institution, operating at arms-length from the government, monitors the economy, sets interest rates, and other such functions. <u>Keeping a population ignorant about their own slavery prevents them from rising up to end it</u>. In this regard, **John Adams**, the 2nd President of the United States, clearly understood what the duplicity of the banking system did to the nation when he reflected,

"There are two ways to conquer and enslave a nation. One is by the sword. The other is by debt."

In most countries, the Reserve Bank has done this very successfully, by providing a continuous inflow of massive capital into the pockets of its **private shareholders**. This gave this small group the financial means to become owners of major segments of the country's economy, and thereby also enabled them to assert a disproportional amount of influence on the government.

Any thinking person who **cares** about the world we live in, and examines it from a "**moral perspective**," <u>would inevitably come to realize how the current pernicious banking system uses its power to enslave us all</u>. The banks, for all their sponsorships and rhetoric about helping the community, in reality, care more about their bottom line than about the people they fleece. They do this not only by the *"Fractional Reserve System,"* but also by their control on setting interest rates, fees and other bank charges. Any wonder that the largest buildings in most countries are the Bank Towers! As decent people who care, how have citizens allowed themselves to be manipulated by an insidious banking system that seems totally oblivious to the fact that, 2% of the population owns 50% of the planet's wealth, where 34,000 die every day because of poverty and preventable diseases, and where half the world's population lives on less than R18 or $2 a day.

Are we so seduced by materialism that we have become less moral? The road to end the exploitation of the banking system and thereby end our own slavery is not going to be an easy one, especially, when more recently governments have also been co-opted into the Bank's nefarious network. One thing we can be sure of, and that is, if we eradicate the Reserve Bank from our monetary structures, our government, and we the taxpayers will not only be out of debt, but as Sir Josiah Stamp said, we would have a better and happier world. One very tangible solution towards ameliorating or possibly even ending South Africa's poverty situation, indeed the poverty of many countries, is to close down the "privately-owned" Reserve Banks that are enslaving citizens, and **demand from the private shareholders of the Reserve Bank that all the stolen assets be returned to the people.**

We have a model where the government by-passed the Reserve Bank and the country came out of debt. During the American Civil War, when President Abraham Lincoln wanted a loan, the European banks offered him the money at the usurious interest rate of 36%. Discovering the fraudulent mechanizations of the Reserve Bank that only enriched its own private members, President Lincoln strongly favored the abolishment of the Reserve Bank and declared:

> *"The government should create, issue and circulate all the currency. Creating and issuing money is the supreme prerogative of government. Adopting these principles would save the taxpayer immense sums of interest, and money will cease to be the master and become the servant of humanity."*

Hence he decided to by-pass the Central Bank. (i.e. the Reserve Bank of that time.) Unfortunately all the money in circulation belonged to the Central Bank. To overcome this problem, Lincoln printed the new government money in green ink to differentiate it from the Central Bank's notes in circulation which were printed in black ink. Hence, the name **"Greenback"** for the new notes. With no interest to pay on the money the Government printed and controlled, the country very quickly got out of debt. The only other time the U.S was out of debt was under President Andrew Jackson in 1835, when he shut down the Central Bank. That bank was the precursor to the Federal Reserve Bank, which as it is presently constituted, was established in 1913 when **President Wilson** approved the Federal Reserve Act. This Act, ultimately led to the concentration of control of America's money in the few men who came to dominate the privately-owned banks.

In South Africa, as a private body owned by its selected **private**

shareholders, (and now a small share held by the Government), the Reserve Bank is a "**cash-cow**" that enriches its private shareholders. This enables them to gain a disproportionate ownership of the country's resources and industries, and thereby continue the exploitation of South Africa's previously cheap labor force – even in the post-apartheid era. This is noted in the numerous labor strikes across the country.

Shortly after Lincoln's government created the "greenback" currency to get out of the clutches of the Central Bank, an **internal document** circulated between the private British and American bankers clearly exposes their plan and intentions. It shows their concern about their loss of control and their determination to re-establish their authority to issue and control the nation's currency. The internal document reads:

> *"Slavery is but the owning of labor and carries with it the care of laborers, while the European plan ... is that capital shall control labor by controlling wages. This can be done by controlling the money. It will not do to allow the greenback, as we cannot control that."*
>
> –*The Hazard Circular, July 1862* [21]

It is worth noting that the Reserve Bank of South Africa, and the Reserve Banks of many other countries, have successfully achieved their goal of *controlling the money* to generate maximum profits for their **private shareholders**, but at great cost to the citizens of the respective countries.

11. IS THE RESERVE BANK PRACTICE A FORM OF MODERN SLAVERY?

People have to work to pay off debt. As interest is **compounded**, they have to work harder to meet the debt payment over and above other payments. This keeps the wage-dependent "slave" in line, powering an empire that only benefits the elite at the top of the pyramid.

"*Physical slavery* requires people to be housed and fed. *Economic slavery* requires the people to feed and house themselves. ... It is one of the most ingenious scams for social manipulation ever created, and at its core, it is an invisible war against the population. **Debt** is the <u>weapon</u> used to conquer and enslave societies, and **interest** is its <u>prime ammunition</u>. .... As the majority walk around oblivious to this reality, the banks, in collusion with governments and corporations, continue to perfect and expand their tactics of economic warfare, spawning new bases such as the **World Bank** and the **International Monetary Fund**." [22]

12. THE ROLE OF THE RESERVE BANK TO CREATE BOOM AND BUST CYCLES

What citizens have to realize is that the Reserve Bank asserts tremendous power in which way the country's economy would go. It has the power to <u>create inflation</u> or <u>a depression</u> by the way it either *increases* the capital in the public domain, or proceeds to *shrink* it.

The reason for creating these states of economic growth and depression or boom and bust cycles are very subtle and sinister. By **lowering interest rates**, a "boom" situation is created as lots of money is pumped into the money supply chain. This positive economic outlook encourages industries to borrow money to expand their businesses, which in turn increases employment. A general feeling of confidence is generated in the flourishing economy that provides workers with a sense of job security. This spurs consumers to take advantage of the bank's low interest rate to purchase bigger homes or renovate their existing dwellings, buy cars or take out big loans to pay for their children's high university fees, or, simply take their families for those long delayed vacations.

Having first flooded the economy with its new easy-made money created from nothing, it now sends out rumblings of inflation creeping in for the purpose of shrinking the money supply for its own advantage. Again, the game-plan is very subtle. Through their networks, hints are given that the Reserve Bank would need to increase the interest rate substantially. Media analysts now start speculating about the number of basis points the interest rate will be hiked. In this way, the media is co-opted to help "<u>prime</u>" the public's **expectation** for such an increase. When the Reserve Bank finally announces the new interest rate, often the hike is not as substantial as the media analysts had speculated. Through this carefully orchestrated game-plan, the Bank is successfully able to obtain from the public both a general sigh of relief as well as acceptance of the new interest rate increase. This Reserve Bank strategy is played out over and over again as the interest rates are increased slowly but incrementally at regular intervals. As is seen in South Africa in the more recent past (2008), these interest increases can easily reach double digit figures. [23]

The outcome of these interest hikes is very predictable. Industries are often the first casualty. As these high interest rates take their toll, industries in financial difficulties usually get bought out, close down or entrench substantial numbers of their workers creating massive unemployment. Those who had borrowed money from the Banks to buy a bigger home, buy a car or renovate their existing dwelling find themselves in situations where they cannot repay their loans and face foreclosures or repossession of their purchased items.

Note how cunningly this boom and bust cycle handsomely rewards the Bankers and impoverishes the citizens by transferring their hard earned assets and properties to the Bank through foreclosures and repossessions.

The question that is usually not asked is whether these Bank foreclosures can **be valid** and **be enforced** if there is an aspect of **fraud?** Consider, under the *Fractional Reserve System* used by the Bank, it did **not actually put out any money** towards the loan of that house other than make a paper entry on its liability sheet. In this instance, there is no *(concrete)* "consideration" and therefore no "risk" taken by the Bank in advancing this supposedly "abstract" loan. If no actual money is withdrawn from the Bank's vault towards that loan, then the home owner making those monthly installment payments is not in reality paying off a **real debt** the Bank has incurred.

That being the case, when the home-owner who is unable to make those Bank payments because he is now unemployed, he is not in any way diminishing the Bank's reserves because no actual money was outlaid in the first place. In fact, whatever payments the home-owner has thus far made in "hard-earned" real money is **sheer profit** for the Bank. This is so because the loan made to the home-owner was simply a mere "liability entry" on the Bank's book sheet. To enforce a foreclosure on an owner's home in such a situation would not only be immoral but also blatantly **fraudulent**, as it would be a **devious means** to transfer to the Bank the property of a hard working citizen.

It is common knowledge that any contract or agreement that is immoral or **fraudulent** in intent or purpose is invalid and cannot be **enforced**. That being the case, would foreclosures where no Bank money is outlaid not be considered invalid as they are inherently fraudulent?

The creation of conditions of a recession or a depression is a crafty way for the Bank owners to cause industries to go bankrupt. And who are the ones who are going to purchase those companies at fire-sale prices? Often it is the behind-the-scene private members and associates of the Reserve Bank, or other financiers who have amassed huge amounts of capital, or those who are given advance knowledge of the increase and decrease of interest rates. In this way, ownership of the economy is further <u>concentrated</u> in the hands of the small group of financial elites.

Most people, including many Americans, are not aware that it was the Federal Reserve Bank of the U.S. that created the **Great Depression of 1929** by contracting the money supply, which resulted in massive mortgage defaults, farm foreclosures and bankruptcies. Milton Friedman, the Nobel-prize winning economist acknowledged this fact in 1996.

We now know that it was Paul Warburg, the father of the Reserve Bank, through a secret advisory, gave **prior notice** to the **private owners** of the Federal Reserve Bank to pull out of the market <u>before the collapse was calculatingly engineered</u>. Many of the viable industries that went bankrupt during this depression were quickly gobbled up at unbelievably low prices by the **private owners** of the Federal Reserve Bank, who were overflowing with cash in their hands because of Warburg's secret advisory notice.

J.P. Morgan, typifies a banker who profited from such crises. "In both banking panics of 1893 and 1907, he intervened, creating the illusion of economic stability while consolidating wealth for his company. J.P. Morgan also benefitted from the Great Depression. When 'Black Thursday' hit in 1929, he bought up cheap stocks to 'keep the economy afloat.' While people endured extreme hardship, J.P. Morgan walked away with significant financial gains.

"Today Morgan's strategy lives on in Chase and CitiGroup ...

these banking **powerhouses** were largely responsible for the most recent economic collapse. They were well aware of their destructive behaviour but did nothing to stop it. In the end, these banks were bailed out **by taxpayer debt** and gained huge profits, while their competitors went under and people lost their homes, jobs, and retirement funds ... this was no accident – it was an intentional power and money grab that has happened throughout the course of history." [24]

More recently, on May 12, 2011, a top European banker, **Oswald J. Grüber,** *(Group Chief Executive Officer, UBS AG Zurich)* speaking at the 41st University of St. Gallen Symposium in Switzerland, admitted, "**We Engineered the Global Financial Crisis.**" [25]

One needs only to examine the recent behaviour of our own South African Reserve Bank's interest hikes, occurring at a time when the country most needed relief from these high interest rates. The explanation given was that it was necessary to fight inflation.

This is absolute nonsense! Increasing the interest rate increases the price of goods and services; it does not decrease it. The common example given to high school students to explain inflation is: "During normal periods, a handful of money would buy a basketful of goods. In inflationary times, a basketful of money is required to buy a handful of goods." Every high school student must have wondered at the disingenuousness of the **Governor of the Reserve Bank** at that time, who explained that hiking interest rates was necessary to curb inflation. [26]

The Governor's explanation to hike interest rates was extremely Machiavellian. In fact, what it did was to have the opposite effect of exacerbating inflation and worsening the financial situation. And this it did very successfully. The Reserve Bank action hit hardest on the **poor**, as the interest hikes increased the prices of goods and services, and caused massive job losses and home foreclosures. But then, the Reserve Bank is not an institution that cares about the citizens of the country, especially the poor. Recessionary-like times are good for the power elite of the Reserve Bank, as it offers them with opportunities to increase their stranglehold on the economy of the country. Their success is guaranteed by society's apathy and indifference. To counteract against the rapacious actions of the private owners of these Banks, individuals must take heed of the advice offered by Sir Josiah Stamp and take responsibility to end their own slavery. Also, citizens may do well to remember what **Plato** said about "apathy":

> *"The price men pay for indifference to public affairs is to be ruled by evil men."* (– or evil bankers?)

We are so side-tracked by other, seemingly more immediate bread and butter issues that we fail to realize the root cause of much of our economic crises may be the Banking system. It has calculatingly created the situation where we are all placed in perpetual debt. Some prudent people may not have individual debts, but as citizens, we all bear a share of the national debt – owed to the Reserve Bank or its agents operating as the World Bank or the IMF. It may be worth reflecting that while the feudal system held humans in physical bondage, the financial elites of modern times, through their Banking institutions, have successfully enslaved the majority of the people economically without them being aware of their own enslavement. This is so aptly captured in the words of **Johann Wolfgang von Goethe** (1749-1832) who reminded citizens that,

> *"None are more hopelessly enslaved than those who falsely believe they are free."*

President Eisenhower, in his farewell speech warned the American citizens about the **military industrial complex** taking control of America and the need for them to be vigilant. *(In South Africa, it is the mining-financial-military-industrial complex that is taking control of the country.)* It would appear there is a conjunction between the military-industrial complex and the Reserve Banks. They form what some call the "Invisible Government." There is strong speculation that President Eisenhower's warning came after an audit of Fort Knox *(the vault where America's gold deposits are stored)*, revealed that most of the gold stored there is now **owned by the private shareholders of the Federal Reserve Bank**, taken as collateral for the American national debt owed to the Federal Reserve Bank. While all government departments are required to have regular audits, it is a known fact that since the audit of Fort Knox during the time of Eisenhower, **there has not been another audit since then about the "ownership" of the gold stored there.** The reason? It appears no President after Eisenhower has the courage to tell the American people that most of the gold stored at Fort Knox no longer belongs to the American people.

Citizens of South Africa, and of course citizens of other countries, would do well to heed the words of President Andrew Jackson, and take the appropriate action to avoid a future of economic enslavement for themselves and their children. After shutting the Central Bank, *(equivalent of the present Federal Reserve Bank)* and taking America out of debt, **President Andrew Jackson** offered this warning:

> *"The bold efforts the present bank has made to control the government are but premonitions of the fate that awaits the American people should they be deluded into a perpetuation of this institution or the establishment of another like it."*

"Unfortunately his message was short-lived, and the international bankers succeeded to install another central bank in 1913 ... *The Federal Reserve Bank.* And as long as this institution exists, <u>perpetual debt</u> is guaranteed." [27]

In this post-apartheid period, there is a small window of opportunity available to **re-structure** institutions like the **South African Reserve Bank** that is doing enormous harm to the citizens of the country, and also greatly impeding the desired economic transformation of the country – **especially to meet the needs of the poor**. The urgency to address these concerns is best underscored by what U.S. **President Thomas Jefferson** said in reference to the Federal Reserve Bank:

> *"If the American people ever allow private banks to control the issue of their currency, first by inflation, then by deflation, the banks... will deprive the people of all property until their children wake-up homeless on the continent their fathers conquered... The issuing power should be taken from the banks and restored to the people, to whom it properly belongs."*

If South Africa, and the majority of other countries who also have privately-owned Reserve Banks are to heed President Jefferson's warning, then the Reserve Banks <u>in their present form</u> need to be abolished. The citizens must demand a return of all those ill-gotten gains made by private shareholders, and re-structure the institution to serve the people – much like the Judiciary that is at arm's length from the government but <u>responsible to Parliament</u>. In this way, the new institution, owned by the people, would ensure that the money created by this institution will:

- **not be used** to enrich a select group of "private" shareholders;
- **end the scheme** where "private" shareholders use the Reserve Bank's profits to increase their own acquisition of the country's valuable assets;
- **enable citizens** of the country, instead of private shareholders to benefit from the wealth the bank may legitimately create;
- **bring about the desired transformation** to address the severely neglected needs of the poor and those most marginalized in society.

If a country's government fails to abolish the Reserve Bank as it is <u>presently structured</u>, its citizens will live to regret it just as **President Woodrow Wilson** did who approved the Federal Reserve Act in 1913. In later years he was greatly repentant about his error and lamented:

> *"I am a most unhappy man. I have unwittingly ruined my country. A great industrial nation is controlled by its system of credit. Our system of credit is concentrated. The growth of the nation, therefore, and all our activities are in the hands of a few men. We have come to be one of the worst ruled, one of the most completely controlled and dominated governments in the civilized world - no longer a government of free opinion, no longer a government by conviction and vote of the majority, but a government by the opinion and duress of a small group of dominant men."*

Citizens can only ignore the warnings of President Woodrow Wilson and the other American Presidents at their own peril.

13. A LEGAL PRECEDENT: Jerome Daly vs. The Bank

In **1969**, a Minnesota man, **Jerome Daly**, took the bank which provided him the loan for his house to court for the foreclosure of his home. "His argument was that the mortgage contract required both parties, being he and the bank, each to put up a legitimate form of property for the exchange. In legal language this is called '**consideration**.'

(Consideration:– a contract's basis. A contract is founded on an **exchange** of one form of consideration for another.)

"Mr. Daly explained that the money was, in fact, not the property of the bank, for it was created out of nothing as soon as the loan agreement was signed.

(According to Modern Money Mechanics) "What they *(the banks)* do when they make loans is to accept promissory notes in exchange for credits. ... The reserves are unchanged by the loan transactions. But deposit credits constitute new additions to the total deposits of the banking system.

"In other words, the money doesn't come out of any of their **existing assets**. The bank is simply inventing it, putting up nothing of its own except for a theoretical liability on paper.

"As the court case progressed, the bank's president, Mr. Morgan, took the stand, and in the **judge's personal memorandum**, he recalled that,

"The Plaintiff (bank's president) admitted that it, in combination with the Federal Reserve Bank ... did create ... the money and the credit upon its books by book-keeping entry ... the money and credit first came into existence when they created it ... Mr. Morgan admitted that no United States law or statute existed which gave him the right to do this ... a lawful consideration must exist and be tendered to support the note." "The jury found that there was no lawful consideration and I agree." He also poetically added, 'Only God can create something of value out of nothing."

"And upon that revelation, the **court rejected the bank's claim for foreclosure** and **Daly kept his home**. The implications of this court decision are immense, for every time you borrow money from a bank, whether it is a mortgage loan or a credit card charge, the money given to you is not only **counterfeit**, it is an illegitimate form of consideration and hence **voids the contract to repay** ... for the bank never had the money as property to begin with. Unfortunately, such legal realizations are suppressed and ignored, and the game of perpetual wealth transfer and perpetual debt continues." [28]

However, once made aware of this scam, it would be a travesty of justice if the country's Courts were to become accomplices by not giving due consideration to the Bankers' game-plans. The high-powered lawyers the Bankers hire are tasked to ensure that perpetual wealth transfer is not in any way hampered by "legalities," even though their schemes are fraudulent and immoral, and they put vast numbers of citizen-victims in a state of perpetual debt. It is therefore imperative that Judges will take serious heed of the precedent set by *Jerome Daly vs. the Bank* when future foreclosure cases are brought before the Courts.

14. ALTERNATIVE MODELS TO THE RESERVE BANK

The concern that is often raised is that there is **no alternative that can replace** the institution of the Reserve Bank as we know it. That is not true. Here are a few models a "People's Central/Reserve Bank" can consider and modify it to best meet each individual country's particular needs.

The early American colonies for example created a <u>fiat-based</u> **interest-free** currency called "**Colonial Scrip**" which was very successful. *(A "fiat-based" currency is simply based on people's faith in its value.)*

> "Just enough money was printed and circulated to facilitate full commerce and prosperity **without paying interest** to central bankers. <u>There was no debt to be repaid</u> – the colonies simply created more money when it was needed, making sure it was spent or lent into existence at the same rate as the real economic growth of goods and services. The Colonial Scrip was eventually **shut down by the British government when they realized the threat of widespread prosperity and independence that it posed.**" [29]

However, it is true that a *fiat-based system* can only be successful if there is a very stringent accounting of the distribution, as well as very careful, responsible and transparent management of the money. But then, is that not a prerequisite for **all** banking matters to avoid abuse!

One of the best example of a successful **inflation-proof, interest-free, Government issued** currency is found on the small island of Guernsey which is about 75 miles south of Great Britain.

> "For almost 200 years, the government of Guernsey has been issuing **interest-free money without causing inflation.** The money supply has gone up about 25 times its

original size, but the economy has remained strong and prosperous. Guernsey is one of the only countries where Central bankers or governments have not dismantled the alternative money system." [30]

One cannot help but compare the interest-free Guernsey currency to the interest-based dollar controlled by the Federal Reserve Bank. While the Guernsey currency is substantially protected from inflation, as pointed out earlier, since the **Federal Reserve Bank** came into existence in 1913, the rate of inflation has caused the American dollar to be devalued by as much as 96%. In other words, the American dollar of 1913 is today worth only 4 cents.

A currency, called the **Liberty Dollar,** backed 100% by gold and silver was created in 1998 as an alternative to the Reserve Bank money. It was introduced by a private non-profit organization, named NORFED (National Organization for the Repeal of the Federal Reserve Act and the Internal Revenue Code).

> "The liberty coins, paper, or digital receipts were redeemable for gold or silver that was stored in a warehouse in Idaho, where it was monitored and audited monthly. This currency held its value over time and quickly claimed a circulation of **$20 million**, making it the second most popular American currency after Federal Reserve Notes. **In 2007, the government raided the group's six warehouses and offices, confiscating the reserves and computers, claiming the coins were illegal because "they could be confused with U.S. coins."** [31]

It would appear that the main reason for the confiscation of the "Liberty Dollar" was not because it would create confusion with the U.S. coins; but rather, that the Liberty Dollar had *"real"* value compared to the *"diminishing value"* of the Reserve Bank currency. The owners of the Reserve Bank could not allow the "Liberty Dollar" to kill their **golden goose** and so in 2007 got the government **to act on their behalf** and do the dirty work of raiding the warehouses of the Liberty Dollar and confiscate their assets. Who benefitted by this Government action on behalf of the Reserve Bank? Certainly not the American citizens!

However, if there are still doubts about alternative models to the Reserve Bank, then consider the **Debt Free** Italian **"Simec,"**

A. Motiar

introduced in 2000 by a wealthy Italian Professor, Giacinto Auriti. The success of the Simec should convince everyone that an **interest free currency** is not only possible but that it also has the advantage of holding its value and thereby arrest inflation.

> "Professor Giacinto Auriti issued a debt-free alternative currency, called **Simec**, and offered it to the people in the small town of Guardiagrele, Italy. The Simecs were a huge success. People discovered that one Simec had twice the purchasing power of the Lire and were eager to shop with the alternative currency. 2.5 billion Simecs circulated rapidly. This program needed a wealthy benefactor to get it going, but it still shows the great potential of debt-free currency to facilitate economic growth and prosperity." [32]

If a wealthy benefactor could successfully get the debt-free "Simec" going, it would be far more straightforward, far simpler, and far more uncomplicated for a **national government** to introduce its own debt-free currency to facilitate economic growth and prosperity.

The above models demonstrate that **viable alternatives do exist** to the exploitative operations of the Reserve Bank as it is presently constituted. To change the status quo, all sectors in society need to play their role to bring about reform:

- It is up to **Citizens** to demand a reform of the present Reserve Bank model which keeps citizens as "slaves" in perpetual debt to the bankers, and by this means, have a stranglehold on the economy of the country which prevents true transformation.
- It is up to national **Governments** to consider abolishing the present form of the *Reserve Bank* in their countries that operate as "**private**" institutions and serve the best interests of their shareholders, rather than those of the citizens or the government.
- It is up to the **Judges** to show moral rectitude when foreclosure orders are brought to court. For justice to prevail, Judges must closely examine the Bank's "*Fractional Reserve System*" and "*securitization*" schemes, which are unjust, fraudulent, cause inflation, devalue the

worth of the country's currency, and have a direct impact on foreclosure cases.

It is imperative to remember, that in the **"Higher Court,"** all mortals, (including Judges) shall be held accountable for all their actions throughout life. That being so, Judges who grant Banks the order to foreclose on clients who are in arrears with their mortgage payments, shall, in that Higher Court, be deemed to have become **accomplices** in the Banks' fraud, if those Judges, before passing judgment, failed to investigate if that homeowner's mortgage had been "securitized" by the Bank.

15. SECURITIZATION

Securitization is the practice of Banks to bundle many loans together as "**securities,**" and then sell these bundles to investors. These securities may comprise of loans, bonds, or mortgages, and are **insured** should debtors not make their payments. Once a person's mortgage loan is "**sold,**" this means that the Bank *(the Mortgagee),* is **fully paid** for that person's mortgage. Hiding this fact from the borrower *(the Mortgager),* the Bank **still requires the Mortgager to continue** making payments to the Bank for the total amortization period *(15 to 25 years),* even though it no longer holds the borrower's mortgage. Aside from the immorality and even illegality of such a practice, this securitization scam immediately raises several questions:

1. Does this not mean that by using this securitization scam, the Bank is getting paid **twice** for one's home mortgage?
2. If the Bank has **sold** a person's mortgage, (with several other mortgages without their knowledge or permission) as a "security" to investors, does it not mean that the Bank is therefore no longer the holder of that homeowner's mortgage?
3. If the Bank no longer holds the homeowner's mortgage, does this not mean that the homeowner is therefore no longer indebted to the Bank because it has been fully paid when it sold that mortgage?
4. Is the Bank not engaging in **fraud** by not letting the homeowner know that it has been **fully paid** when it sold the mortgage to investors, but still require the homeowner to continue making payments for that **paid-up** mortgage?
5. If the Bank no longer holds the homeowner's mortgage when it sold it to investors, then why is the Bank allowed to foreclose on the homeowner when he misses some payments because of unforeseen circumstances?

The only person, who possibly might have a claim on the

homeowner's mortgage payments, is the **investor**, who purchased this mortgage in a bundle with other debts as an **insured** "security". However, the investor's claim may lack legitimacy because the mortgage is purchased from the Bank without the knowledge or permission of the **original owner** of that mortgage.

In any case, the investor is usually **not** interested to know the individual defaulting mortgager because,

(a) the total "bundle of mortgage securities" is insured, and

(b) it may be a long drawn-out process to identify, which mortgagee amongst the many in the bundle is in default with his payments. It is for these reasons that these **"insured securities,"** under this securitization scam are often referred to as **"junk bonds"**.

16. BENEFITS IF THE RESERVE BANK IS ABOLISHED

Let's consider the benefits to citizens if the Reserve Bank, as it is presently structured is abolished and replaced by a "Central Bank of the People":

1. A *Central Bank of the People* which operates using a **debt-free currency** would not have its value diminish at the rate at which it is presently done under the existing Reserve Bank model.

2. Most important of all, "**Privately-owned**" **Reserve Banks** are the biggest obstacle to citizen empowerment. No country can hope to achieve even a nominal degree of **transformation** to alleviate the financial conditions of the poor and the marginalized in society, if they remain beholden to the "privately-owned" Reserve Banks. Consider the wealth-making power the South African government has given away to the **privately-owned** Reserve Banks to make its own citizens **debt-slaves**.

    > "Since 2000 the SARB [South African Reserve Bank] probably printed about 100 billion Rand out of thin air. This allowed the commercial banks to use about R40 billion to fractionally leverage at about 40:1 and create about R1.6 trillion in additional money out of thin air. (That's R1,600,000,000,000)

    > "We can see that while the SARB printed R100 billion out of nothing, the commercial banks created about R1.6 trillion **out of nothing** by crediting customer accounts with digital currency and then charging interest on the money they created out of nothing." [33]

    The chart below [34] shows graphically the exponential growth of the South African Bank's assets since 2000, which were leveraged from just **R100 billion** to the colossal total of **R1.6 trillion**. (This amount is so massive that if one were to count 1.6 trillion in seconds, it would take more than 50,000 years to do so!) [35] This massive amount created by the fractional reserve system, provides legitimacy to the widespread view that whoever controls the creation of money controls the government, and also controls the economy. The grave injustice of this monetary system is that it transfers to Banks the wealth that should belong to the citizens. This further impoverishes the masses and widens the gap between the rich and the poor.

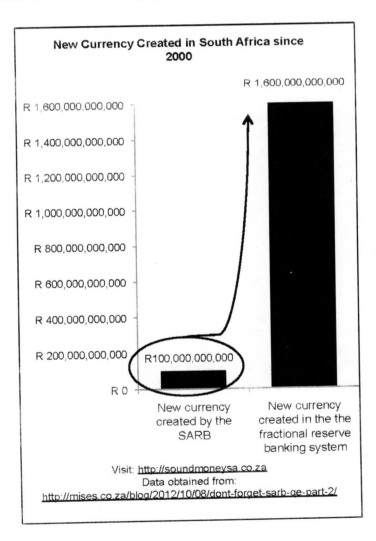

With this kind of financial stranglehold, the citizens of the country, including their government, will forever remain enslaved to the Bankers, and therefore will never have enough money to meet the needs of the population. Hence, the only solution is to abolish or nationalize the Reserve Bank and the other Banks which accumulate huge balances using the fractional reserve banking system, and let all their assets be returned to the government on behalf of the citizens who were massively ripped off.

3. The *Central Bank of the People* would not have to pay **R70,000 per meeting** to its Directors as is done by the present Reserve Bank, which is obviously flushed with "easy-made" money that rightfully belongs to the citizens of South Africa.

4. The *Central Bank of the People,* by taking over the assets of the present Reserve Bank, would have enough money available to pay for the country's infrastructure and other needs. In South Africa's case, citizens will not have to:
    *   have electricity bills increased so high to make them unaffordable for average income earners;
    *   pay high **e-tolling** fees to upgrade city roads;
    *   pay extra tax to help improve the health care and education systems;
    *   borrow money to meet urgent infra-structure needs of the community, etc.

5. The *Central Bank of the People* can make money available for the government at **no interest** to build low cost houses for the poor who were most marginalized by the apartheid regime.

6. A Committee, made up of ONE member from each political party in Parliament, representatives from at least two major religious groups, and representatives from at least two active non-profit civil society organizations should administer the *Central Bank of the People*. Chairmanship of the Committee or Governorship would be on a bi-annual rotation basis to ensure the Chairperson / Governor does not become over-powerful to over-ride the opinion of other members. Committee members may not serve more than two years. Each year, half its members have to be replaced by new representatives from the same political, religious or civil society group whose term has expired, except for the first year of operation, when half the members would have to be replaced after only one year.

Salaries of Committee members would be what they receive as Members of Parliament, and nominal stipends to the representatives from religious and civil society organizations **if** they are not paid by their own respective groups. There should be no **double dipping** by Committee members.

7. The **expert economic** advisors and **researchers** employed by the Reserve Bank may be replaced **or** retained with a new mandate. Focus of their new mandate would now be on what is best for the **citizens** of the country as opposed to their old mandate which was to increase profits for the Reserve Bank's shareholders.

For additional **benefits**, see Page 64

17. A CONCERN:

Several citizens expressed the concern that the money-lenders/banks are so entrenched and powerful that it would be very difficult to change the status quo. Such an attitude would be tantamount to accepting one's own enslavement to the money-lenders. Individually, the task to bring about change may be daunting, though not impossible. However, there is strength in numbers. Collectively, much can be done to free citizens from the clutches of the privately-owned Reserve Banks and other Banks with their immoral easy-money-making *Fractional Reserve System*, and *"securitization"* schemes. Fortunately, we now have several communities of dedicated people who are seeking reform and transparency in the banking and corporate sector.

In South Africa we have:

"The New Economic Rights Alliance" (NewERA),
www.newera.org.za

In the United States we have:

"The Public Trust 1776 Resurrection of Forgotten Principles"
http://hopegirl2012.wordpress.com/

and

"The THRIVE Movement"
(Foster, Kimberly and the THRIVE team)
http://www.thrivemovement.com/

They have acted on the advice offered by *Margaret Mead* who said:
"Never doubt that a small group of thoughtful committed people, can change the world; indeed, it's the only thing that ever has."

By joining these groups, or forming similar organizations in one's own country, working jointly and co-operatively with each other, **INDIVIDUALS** can unite with millions of others who believe most banking institutions, and many large corporations, are in breach of natural human rights. We can succeed if we start to have faith in the fact that there is "strength in unity," and begin to recognize that "an injury to one is an injury to all"!

18. SPEAKING TRUTH TO POWER:

To stand aloof in the face of injustice is to facilitate oppression. As *individuals*, we have inherent obligations which we sometimes forget to consider. Suppressing the TRUTH makes us all accomplices in the INJUSTICE that is perpetrated against victims. By exposing the truth, we not only liberate ourselves, but also the oppressors. More importantly, we free our conscience from the guilt of silence in the face of power.

Regarding individual responsibility, it is worth remembering that when the fire of Nimrod had engulfed Prophet Abraham, a little frog filled its mouth with water to put out the fire. When others laughed at this seemingly futile act of kindness, the frog reminded them: **"On the day of Judgement, I will be asked what I did within my capacity in the face of this injustice."**

Living in a so-called democracy must not delude us into believing that we live in a society free of injustice. *Ramsey Clark*, former United States Attorney General, quite candidly said,

> *"We're not a democracy. It's a terrible misunderstanding and a slander to the idea of democracy to call us that. In reality, we're a plutocracy: a government by the wealthy."*

No change has ever come about without action. To change the human condition, the economic status quo which keeps the majority of citizens as debt-slaves to the Bankers needs to be transformed. As *individuals*, one must acknowledge that "economic enslavement" is a moral issue. Regarding this moral question, *Dante*, writing during the Renaissance period, puts the choice individuals have in the starkest and most uncompromising terms. Paraphrased, his quote states:

> **"Those who do not take part in a moral controversy, there will be for them, a special place in hell."**

On individual responsibility, let us also not forget the words of *Edmund Burke*, who said:

> **"The only thing necessary for the triumph of evil, is for good men to do nothing."**

19. POSTSCRIPT

New Economic Rights Alliance

supporting victims of corporations that put profit ahead of human rights.

www.newera.org.za

PO Box 102405, Moreleta Plaza, 0167, South Africa
Tel: +27 82 515 1496   Fax: +27 86 241 4391   Email: admin@newera.org.za

The New Economic Rights Alliance's Constitutional Court Case aims to obtain transparency in banking.

The following outlines the reasons behind our action:

1. Banks do not "loan" money as their prolific advertisements claim. Money loaned is actually money created, via an elaborate scheme of paper shifting and number crunching. This involves the use of loan application forms and negotiable instruments, the result being debit and credit book entries that have no liquid money value. It can be said that banks make money out-of-thin-air under the "pretence" of a loan, but in reality it is not a loan at all. This is deceptive and misleading as very few South Africans know the truth.

2. It is a common legal principle in our law that one must possess that which one loans. For reasons above, the banks are unable to meet this, a fundamental criteria for a valid borrower / lender contract.

3. Banks are failing to provide simple information to their customers that should be easy to access. Examples include a certificate of balance, audited proof that a lawful "deposit" was actually made and the physical location of original documents, promissory notes and other negotiable instruments. Instead of providing the customer with this information, they choose to take legal action, and foreclose on homes and assets with remarkable alacrity.

4. The banks are acting as intermediary / agent between the customer and other parties. It is a requirement that an agency relationship be fully disclosed up front to the customer. The banks do not disclose this relationship and, as a result, most people are under the complete illusion that they are borrowing from their bank in the ordinary sense of the word.

5. Banks engage in a widespread and common practice called **securitization**. Instead of borrowing from the Reserve Bank on our behalf, banks bundle many loans together and then sell these bundles to investors whereby the loans become securities. This process caused the stock market crash of 2008 and threatens the global economy as we speak. In fact, the betting game being played by the banks, called the derivatives market, is currently estimated to be 20 times larger than the GDP of the entire planet. Rather than slowing down, its sheer propensity for profit has led to a rampant growth of the industry in South Africa. The Bank Act makes it crystal clear that securitization falls outside the business of a bank. Therefore, it is a blatant breach of the Bank Act for a bank to engage in this practice, and rightly so.

6. Banks refuse to disclose the securitization process to the customer, who has a legal right to this information. When a customer asks for disclosure, the banks do not even bother responding, or respond using unintelligible legal jargon. The entire securitization process is kept tightly secret while it provides huge profits to those behind the scenes. Instead of securitization providing a benefit to the customer by way of lower interest rates, the reverse occurs: banks swiftly and relentlessly foreclose on assets in order to satisfy the needs of their investors. It should also be mentioned that banks have been known to securitize a debt several times, and that should a person default those investors are protected by an insurance policy.

7. We have written confirmation from the South African Reserve Bank that, once a bank sells a loan into a securitization pool, they lose the legal right to that asset. This means that literally tens, if not hundreds of thousands of homes and other assets have been taken away from South Africans illegally because the wrong entity is suing in court.

8. Banks do not use "money," they use negotiable instruments. These instruments are defined clearly in the Bills of Exchange Act and have been used by trading merchants for thousands of years. It is the constitutional right of every South African to have an explanation of how our instruments are being used, traded, and exploited by the banks.

9. Banks are foreclosing on people's homes and assets by using the contract as a shield. Their argument is simple: "you signed a contract, so you must pay." By sticking to the age old axiom: the-agreement-is-king, anyone attempting to look behind the shield is prohibited from doing so. This loan agreement, which is a series of one-way payments with absolutely no risk whatsoever to the bank, is somehow enough to allow them to win in court. We believe that granting summary judgment in such a manner, without the courts listening to the counter argument that the contract is not valid due to malicious deception, is unconstitutional.

10. It is illegal for banks to claim more than double the amount loaned from any borrower (the in duplum rule). However, banks are not only breaking this rule, but they are also forcing people to pay the interest on loans up front. In other words, the interest is paid back first, before the principal. This is plainly illegal.

11. The collection processes in banks have become so extreme, that call centre operators have been known to verbally abuse customers. The customer believes, quite wrongly, that the bank is running at a loss and is simply doing its best to get its money back. This illusion is maintained by the banks who continue to refine their well-oiled, clinical machine of repossession and foreclosure.

12. If a bank employee dispenses with an affidavit, it is a legal requirement that the directors of that bank first dispense with a Special Resolution granting permission for that employee to make such an affidavit. This rule is currently being circumvented. Somehow, half-hearted affidavits, made by just about anyone in the bank, are being successfully used to obtain judgment and foreclosures.

13. When a bank makes a deposit, they are prescribed by law to adhere to certain administrative procedures outlined in the

Banks Act. This is to ensure that the required liquidity procedures are adhered to. Banks are circumventing these procedures and are engaging in unlawful deposits, placing the economy of the entire country at risk.

14. There is an overall sense of conduct and legal justice required for the good of the community (boni mores). By opting to merely rubber stamp orders during Summary Judgment (a process which has been called a "draconian measure" by our very own honorable Judges), without so much as even testing these arguments, the courts and banks are tearing down the very fabric of the Constitution.

15. The legal relationship between a bank and its customer is fiduciary, not dissimilar to that of a doctor and his patient, an estate agent and a home owner or a lawyer and her client. By engaging in secret and underhanded dealings, and by not disclosing the full truth up front, the banks are taking full advantage of their customers in the name of profiteering. As such, this fiduciary relationship has been broken which is a most grave and serious crime. This crime is perpetuated when the principal fails to answer, and even bluntly ignores the requests and pleas of their customer in their hour of need.

16. Finally, it is a constitutional right for a person to have a full and fair trial. This right is being circumvented by the courts in favor of swift and harsh Summary Judgments, leading to the loss of assets and homes.

BENEFITS:

Should this action be successful, what is the benefit for the average Citizen?

1. Interest rates and fees could be reduced, thus significantly reducing monthly repayments.

2. Banks will become more forgiving when dealing with defaulters, possibly even taking out an insurance policy to protect the customer.

3. Forced austerity measures, currently being implemented in several countries around the world, could be reduced or even avoided here in South Africa.

4. Courts will have more freedom to expand the common law, providing a stronger and fairer defense for South Africans

wishing to save their homes. Currently, the banks are ruling the courts and this has got to change.

5.   There will be a more competitive choice when loaning money or purchasing a home, as banks will be disallowed to act outside the competition legislation.

6.   Secrecy in dealing with a client's money and loan agreements will be a matter of the past, thus transparency shall prevail and people will know the inner workings of the banking system once and for all.

7.   Additional stock options should also be available whereby the client can elect to purchase back or extend its borrowings on the open market or through securitization packages. This alternative form of financing will greatly help to prevent their assets from being taken away.

For justification for the above contentions, and an on-going discussion of the case, visit
www.thebigcase.co.za

For more information go to:

1.   *NewERA Blog* http://www.newera.org.za/
2.   *Bold Activists Reveal Strategies for fighting Home Foreclosures and balancing your Government's budget*

   http://www.thrivemovement.com/bold-actiivists-reveal-strategies-for-fighting-home-foreclosures-and-balancing-government-budget.blog

20. 10 QUESTIONS EVERYONE SHOULD ASK THEIR BANK

New Economic Rights **Alliance** (NewERA)

supporting victims of corporations that put profit ahead of human rights

www.newera.org.za

The NewERA highly recommends that everyone ask their bank the following 10 questions.

Included are reasons why, in our opinion, the banks refuse to answer them.

1. *Am I indebted to the bank right now? (Please answer yes or no).*

2. *Please confirm that the bank actually possessed the money they claim to have lent me, prior to my loan being granted. In other words, did the bank physically have the money they lent me, prior to the money appearing in my account?*

3. *Would the bank be prepared to amend the credit agreement as follows? "We, the bank, did in fact possess the money we loaned you, prior to the loan being approved."*

4. *Was the loan funded by assets belonging to the bank at the time the loan was granted? Either way, please describe in detail the accounting process used to create my loan.*

5. *Did the bank record my promissory note / negotiable instrument as an asset on its books? If yes, how was my instrument used to create my loan, and where is my valuable promissory note / negotiable instrument now?*

6. *Does the bank participate in a securitization scheme whereby debts / promissory notes are bundled and then sold-on to a third party/parties via special purpose vehicles, entities or similar processes?*

7. *With reference to point 6, is my loan securitized? If so, please send*

me all the details regarding its securitization.

8. *Does the bank have a legal right to collect money it claims I owe it? If so, then where does this legal right come from, assuming the loan has been securitized?*

9. *Has my loan with the bank been settled by a special purpose vehicle, insurance policy, or by any other party?*

10. *Regarding the security given to the bank by me, has this security been sold or given as security / surety to another party?*

THE 10 QUESTIONS EXPLAINED

1. **Am I indebted to the bank right now? (Please answer yes or no).**

    Obvious question, right? Wrong. In fact, your bank may well refuse to answer it.

    Here's why: If your loan has been **securitized**, then you are no longer indebted to your bank. If you are not indebted to your bank, then in our opinion, the bank cannot take judgement against you.

    A recent judgment in the US (one of many similar judgments since 2008) has ordered banks to pay out US$8.5billion to consumers because of banking fraud. This is almost identical to what NewERA is seeking.

    In the case of securitization, your legal position with the bank has changed. Did your bank disclose securitization to you? Do you even know what it means? Probably not. Therefore, you should seek recourse and together with NewERA we may follow the success of other countries.

    Also, if the bank does answer "yes" to this question, and it turns out that your loan has been securitized, then it is our opinion that the bank has placed itself in a position of fraud and quite possibly perjury. This could lead to criminal action against the bank and possible recourse for you.

2. **Please confirm that the bank actually possessed the money they claim to have lent me prior to my loan being granted. In other words, did the bank physically have the money they lent me, prior to the money appearing in my account?**

    It is unlikely that your bank will answer this question. However, they may try to disguise the answer by using clever language, so read their answer very carefully.

If your loan was securitized, then the bank's money was not used to fund the loan. Therefore, a legitimate loan between you and the bank may not exist. The bank could never admit this, because to do so would be to admit that there could not possibly be a loan agreement with you.

Even if your loan was not securitized, then the bank still cannot answer this question. Why? Because the bank did not loan you their own lawful money. Something you need to know about banking: banks do not "loan" money in the ordinary sense of the word. This is a tricky concept, and works like this:

Banks do not make loans. Instead, they "advance" or "extend" something called "credit." This simply means that a magical facility is created that provides you with "money" that is made out of thin air. As hard as it is for you to accept this, the money loaned to you was simulated (i.e. virtual).

To illustrate: A customer deposits R100 into their bank. The bank then quickly makes nine photocopies of that R100. They lend those photocopies to nine people, charging interest on each of those so-called loans. Then, if the loan is not paid back with interest, they take away the assets pledged as security.

In reality banks do not use a photocopier, they use a computer. The loan amount is typed into the computer and, hey presto, "magical" money is created out of thin air. You think that this money is a loan or debt so you feel obligated to pay it back. However, it was never actually *lent* to you in the first place.

3. ***Would the bank be prepared to amend the credit agreement as follows? "We, the bank, did in fact possess the money we loaned you, prior to the loan being approved."***

If NewERA was wrong, then the banks would have no problem complying with this request. However, see for yourself: they will not agree to amend the contract.

If your loan has been securitized, your original agreement is no longer with the bank! A bank loses all right and title to the loan agreement once it has been sold into a securitization scheme. One cannot amend an agreement when they are no longer legally entitled to it, nor do they have it in their possession. Furthermore, any indebtedness to the bank would have been settled as a result of the sale of the asset.

Put simply, no matter what the situation, the bank did not possess the money it loaned you, and never did. They are fooling you and participating in a fraud of monumental proportions. The fraud is that they cannot take away your assets without disclosing the truth to both you and the Court.

4. *Was the loan funded by assets belonging to the bank at the time the loan was granted? Either way, please describe in detail the accounting process used to create my loan.*

If everything is legitimate and above board, then banks should have no problem explaining how your particular loan came into being. However, banks will not reveal this to you. When you ask your bank these questions, you will see for yourself.

You need to know something else about banking: Banks do not deal with actual, physical "money." Instead, they operate with *promises to pay.* For example: if a bank promises to pay you R10,000, that would equate to a R10,000 deposit into your account. This deposit is reflected on your statement as a promise of the bank, to you, for R10,000. In other words, it looks like you have R10,000 in your account, but actually this number merely represents R10,000 worth of promises made by a bank to you.

The words "money" and "deposit" are therefore misleading. The banks redefined these words so they sound the same in everyday use, but mean something very different to the legal and banking system.

Another word being misused is the word "transfer." A *transfer* is not a transfer of money. It is simply a case of the bank shifting their promise to pay "A" to a promise to pay "B." This is only an illusion of a transfer.

Do you remember when you first took out a loan? You gave the bank a promise, in writing, to make payments every month, with interest. This written promise to pay money to the bank becomes the money they used to lend you! Therefore, you actually created your own loan. It takes some time to get your head around this, and we recommend you research the links below to help you understand the process.

5. *Did the bank record my promissory note / negotiable instrument as an asset on its books? If yes, how was my instrument used to create my loan, and where is my valuable*

promissory note / negotiable instrument now?

This question is designed to trick the banks. You want confirmation from your bank that they deal in negotiable instruments (promises). Once admitted, it will confirm most of what NewERA is saying.

Remember, real money (gold and silver, or notes that represent gold and silver) no longer exist. The illusion of money (known as "credit" or "bank promises") quietly replaced real money so that the banks could fund their own business empire by creating money out of nothing, and then charging interest on it.

Negotiable instruments (promissory notes and bills of exchange) serve, in effect, as money. So, when you give the bank a promissory note (a written promise to pay back a loan), they convert *your* promise into *their* promise. Their promise = so called "money." So you gave them the money they loaned you.

6. ***Does the bank participate in a securitization scheme whereby debts / promissory notes are bundled and then sold-on to a third party/parties via special purpose vehicles, entities or similar processes?***

This question is plain and simple: we want the banks to admit the obvious. We know they engage in securitization, but once they admit this to a customer, then the customer would naturally have the right to ask a crisp follow-up question: *"Well then, has my specific loan been securitized?"* Remember, if your loan has been securitized, then the whole game changes. This is ultimately what we want the banks to tell us. South African banks are securitizing around R30 billion per month so there is a very good chance that your loan has been securitized. You need to know the truth, which is why you MUST persist in your demand for answers.

7. ***With reference to point 6, is my loan securitized? If so, please send me all the details regarding its securitization.***

It is your right to know about securitization. If you don't get answers, then work with NewERA to obtain recourse.

The one institution that answers this question in detail is SA Homeloans. This is because SA Homeloans is not a bank. They explain securitization openly and transparently. Now contrast the answers from SA Homeloans with those of the banks who go dead silent when you ask them this question. In some cases, banks will reply by stating that your loan has not been securitized. This is quite rare – usually they just ignore the question. They certainly won't tell you if your loan *has* been securitized. Read the links below for more on securitization – this is very important.

8. ***Does the bank have a legal right to collect money it claims I owe it? If so, then where does this legal right come from, assuming the loan has been securitized?***

The bank only has one counter argument to this: *there is a contract between you and the bank.* However, if your loan has been securitized, the contract is sold! It's gone. The bank no longer has the contract, nor does it have the right to that contract. What part of this do the banks not understand? If a bank alludes or pretends they have it, then we believe that they are committing fraud.

The contract between you and the bank could conceivably say anything it wants to. The fact is that it has been sold and the bank has lost all rights to it. In our opinion, the bank cannot legally, ethically or morally claim back the debt from you because they have already been paid and profited.

9. ***Has my loan with the bank been settled by a special purpose vehicle, insurance policy, or by any other party?***

This is going to shock you, so be warned. When a loan is securitized, your loan gets bundled with other loans and then sold to a third party. If you default (miss a few payments), then the third party (called an SPV – Special Purpose Vehicle) carries insurance. They get paid out if you default!

This needs to be emphasised: If you get sick or lose your job, or you cannot meet your repayment obligations, then the secret third parties who trade in your loans get paid out. They are protected against your default. So then... where is your protection? Nowhere. You have no protection because to protect you would mean to inform you of the game and once you know the game, the game is over.

And one more thing... if the SPV is insured so they get paid out if you default... and the bank was paid for your loan right up front when the loan was securitized. So then... how and why are they able to foreclose on your assets? And where does the money go from the sale on the Sheriff's auction? This is precisely what NewERA is fighting to expose.

A. Motiar

10. ***Regarding the security given to the bank by me, has this security been sold or given as security / surety to another party?***

This is the final nail in the coffin. Put simply, we want the bank to admit that they no longer have your security. If they do not have your security, then they cannot foreclose. The banks will never admit this because it means admitting that trillions of Rand in foreclosures of assets over the past two decades would have been illegal. This would lead to the biggest class action lawsuit of all time... which is happening now, so join NewERA!

The New Economic Rights Alliance NPC. Directors:
SC Cundill, BA Vermaak, GJ Robbertse, DC Moodley, CG Sapsford.

Reference material and additional research:

Securitisation: A conspiracy of Silence
http://www.newera.org.za/wp-content/uploads/2012/11/Securitisation-A-Conspiracy-of-Silence.pdf

SA Banks Must Pay Out Big Time
http://www.newera.org.za/sa-banks-must-pay-out-big-time/

21. Endnotes:

[1] http://rogerdufur.blogspot.com/2013/02/banker-admit-engineer-financial-crisis.html
Oswald J. Grüber, speaking at the 41st Gallen Symposium, May 12-13, 2011, University of St. Gallen, Switzerland: "Panel on the Global Economic Power Shift."

[2] The recent "<u>Basel 3</u>" directive issued to Banks around the world is an indication of the location of this "apex of control".

[3] Glenn Beck Exposes the Private Fed: See Youtube
http://www.youtube.com/watch?v=vB5LKjihgk&feature=endscreen&NR=1

[4] G. Edward Griffin: Author of, *"The Creature from Jekyll Island."*

[5] Professor Carroll Quigley of Georgetown University, highly esteemed by his former student, William Jefferson Blythe Clinton, in *Tragedy and Hope: A History of The World in Our Time* (Macmillan Company, 1966).

[6] Documentary *THRIVE:*
http://www.thrivemovement.com/the_movie

[7] Documentary *THRIVE:*
http://www.thrivemovement.com/the_movie

[8] Documentary *THRIVE:*
http://www.thrivemovement.com/the_movie

[9] *"Zeitgeist Addendum"* transcript from <u>Global Outlook</u>, Collector's Edition, p. 228

[10] Mail & Guardian: 13 April 2012

[11] *"Zeitgeist Addendum"* transcript from <u>Global Outlook</u>, Collector's Edition, p. 227

[12] *"Zeitgeist Addendum"* transcript from <u>Global Outlook</u>, Collector's Edition, p. 227

[13] *"Zeitgeist Addendum"* transcript from <u>Global Outlook</u>, Collector's Edition, p. 227

[14] *"Zeitgeist Addendum"* transcript from <u>Global Outlook</u>, Collector's Edition, p. 227

[15] Mail & Guardian: 13 June, 2008.

[16] Global Outlook, Collector's Edition, *The Tower of Basel – Secretive Plans for issuing a Global Currency*, p. 237

[17] DVD *The Money Masters*: How International Bankers Gained Control of America, Royalty Production Company, 1998-2004

[18] Ibid., DVD *The Money Masters*

[19] <u>Global Outlook</u>, Collector's Edition, *Some Members of the Invisible Government and what they say about their New World Order,* p. 11

[20] <u>Global Outlook</u>, Collector's Edition p. 202

[21] Ibid., p. 229

[22] *"Zeitgeist Addendum"* transcript from Global Outlook, Collector's Edition, p. 229

[23] Mail & Guardian: 12 June, 2008 and 28 July, 2008

[24] Documentary *THRIVE:*
http://www.thrivemovement.com/the_movie

[25] http://rogerdufur.blogspot.com/2013/02/banker-admit-engineer-financial-crisis.html
41st Gallen Symposium, May 12-13, 2011, University of St. Gallen, Switzerland: "Panel on the Global Economic Power Shift."

[26] Mail & Guardian: 23 June, 2008

[27] Global Outlook, Op. cit., p.228

[28] *"Zeitgeist Addendum"* transcript from Global Outlook, Collector's Edition, p. 229

[29] Documentary *THRIVE:*
http://www.thrivemovement.com/the_movie

[30] Documentary *THRIVE:*
http://www.thrivemovement.com/the_movie

[31] Documentary *THRIVE:*
http://www.thrivemovement.com/the_movie

[32] Documentary *THRIVE:*
http://www.thrivemovement.com/the_movie

[33] http://soundmoneysa.co.za/2012/10/the-fed-vs-sarb-in-the-central-banks-print-match/#comment-503]

[34] http://soundmoneysa.co.za/2012/10/the-fed-vs-sarb-in-the-central-banks-print-match/

[35] Hopegirl shows that 1 Trillion seconds equals to approximately 32,000 years:
http://hopegirl2012.files.wordpress.com/2013/02/debt-truth-02.pdf

By the same Author. . .

3E Magic Math Games: Winner of the (Canadian) PRIME MINISTER'S AWARD for Teaching Excellence in Science, Technology and Mathematics. Includes **4** FUN games: ONE Individual Solitaire-type game and THREE popular Group games which are fun for both children and parents. Great to have FUN while improving Math skills!

3E Reading System: The first system to break the so-called reading code in 1980 to enable children to start reading in 12 days. For its success in teaching reading skills so effectively the author was honored with the ACRA Award of Achievement, a VIP Award from the Learning Disabilities Association and a Certificate of Excellence from the York Region Board of Education. The author has also presented the ***3E Reading System*** at National, International and University Conferences

De-fanging a Bully is the first book to offer solutions to for bullying from the perspective of the victim. Bullying will not come to an end by appealing to the "goodwill" of the bully. It will only stop by "**empowering the victim**" and "**de-fanging the bully**" by changing the strategic "power balance" in favour of the victim. Only when victims are empowered and bullies are "defanged" will bullying behaviour come to an end, whether it is school-yard bullying, spousal abuse or work-place intimidation.

Archbishop Edward W. Scott: *"We need more of this kind of literature."*

"I am not Dumb" Endorsed by the **UN Commission for the International Year of the Child**, it explores Learning Disabilities in a **Child's language** and from a **Child's perspective**. Children can sometimes be very cruel, engaging in name calling and teasing. This book helps children gain *empathy* by assisting them to become more tolerant. Also includes practical activities.

Word/Vocabulary "Rummy" Game: Finally, a Word Game that offers the **fun** of the popular Rummy game but also helps to build *vocabulary*. Children *love* it. Parents *enjoy* it. Everybody's *vocabulary* improves and so do their *spelling skills*. What a rewarding way to learn while having great *family fun!*

For more information go to:
www.MathAndLiteracyAfrica.co.za

CPSIA information can be obtained at www.ICGtesting.com
Printed in the USA
BVOW07s1849271013

334763BV00005B/18/P